Magnets

Magnetism

Rachel Lynette

Heinemann Library
Chicago, Illinois

Customer Service 888-454-2279
Visit our website at www.heinemannraintree.com

Designed by Richard Parker and Tinstar Design Ltd, www.tinstar.co.uk
Illustrations by ODI
Printed and bound in China by Leo Paper Group.

12 11 10 09 08
10 9 8 7 6 5 4 3 2 1

Library of Congress Cataloging-in-Publication Data
Lynette, Rachel.
Magnets : magnetism / Rachel Lynette.
p. cm. -- (Do it yourself)
Includes bibliographical references and index.
ISBN 978-1-4329-1097-6 (hc) -- ISBN 978-1-4329-1113-3 (pb) 1. Magnets--Juvenile literature. I. Title.
QC757.5.L96 2008
538′.4--dc22
2008008463

Acknowledgments
The publishers would like to thank the following for permission to reproduce photographs:
©Alamy pp. **7** (Jon Arnold Images Ltd), **9** (JUPITERIMAGES/Comstock Images), **15** (Design Pics Inc.), **40** (Technology And Industry Concepts), **43** (GapysKrzysztof); © Comstock Images p. **38**; ©Corbis pp. **17,25** (zefa/Sagel & Kranefeld), **28** (Sygma/Hashimoto Noboru), **29** (Kevin Fleming), **33** (Michael S. Yamashita), **42** (Solus-Veer); ©DK Images p. **31** (Dave King); ©Getty Images pp. **4** (PHOTO 1/DEA), **21** (VEER John Churchman), **35** (Peter Ginter); ©Pearson Education Ltd pp. **5, 14,** **27** (Tudor Photography); ©Science Photo Library pp. **11** (BSIP Fife), **13**, **19** (Cordelia Molloy), **16** (David Weintraub), **23** (Chris Madeley), **34**; ©TOGRAFOX p. **39** (R. D. Battersby); ©Tom Yuzvinsky, PhD, Postdoctoral Scientist Centre of Integrated Nanomechanical Systems, University of California at Berkeley p. **41**.

Cover photograph of horseshoe magnet with iron filings reproduced with permission of ©Science Photo Library / Tek Image.

The publishers would like to thank Ann Fullick for her help in the preparation of this book.

Every effort has been made to contact copyright holders of any material reproduced in this book. Any omissions will be rectified in subsequent printings if notice is given to the publishers.

Contents

Any words appearing in the text in bold, **like this**, are explained in the glossary.

The Power of Magnets

Magnets come in many different strengths, shapes, and sizes. Some are small, such as the ones you might have on your refrigerator. Other magnets, such as the ones found in recycling plants to sort metal, may be very large and powerful. Magnets can be made into any shape. Some of the more common shapes include bars, circles, doughnuts, and horseshoes.

Magnets were first discovered in ancient China and Greece. The word "magnet" comes from "Magnesia," which was the name of the region in Greece where some of the first magnets were found in 600 BCE. These first magnets were a type of rock called **lodestone**. The ancient Greeks found that small pieces of iron were attracted to lodestones.

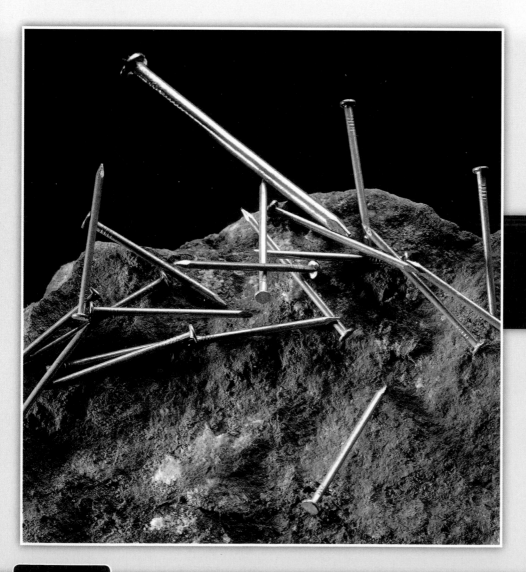

Lodestones like this one are a type of magnet.

Properties of magnets

Most people know that magnets attract metal, but magnets do not attract all kinds of metal. Only certain types of metal are attracted to magnets. Magnets also attract some kinds of **minerals**. Things that are attracted to magnets are called **magnetic materials**.

Every magnet has two **poles**: north and south. The poles are the strongest part of the magnet. Opposite poles attract each other—they are pulled toward each other. Poles that are the same **repel**, which means that they push away from each other.

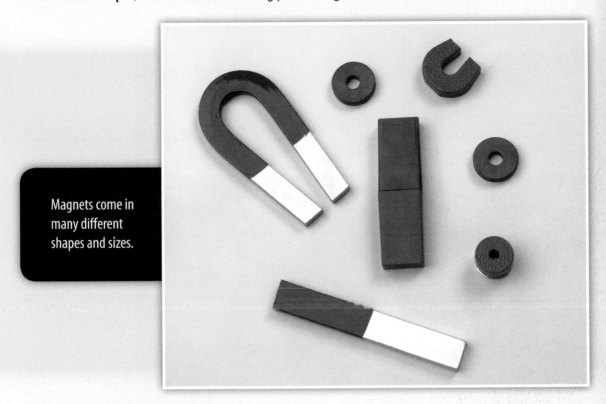

Magnets come in many different shapes and sizes.

Taking care of your magnets

Magnets can get damaged or broken. Do not drop magnets or strike them with a hard object. Keep them away from heat. These things can weaken the magnet's strength.

Magnets can be stored together with opposite sides touching. They should never be stored with like sides touching or near each other. It is also a good idea to put a metal strip across the poles of your magnets.

Magnets can also cause damage to things around you. Keep magnets away from computers, video or audiotapes, and wind-up watches. The magnets can damage these devices. Also be sure to keep your magnets away from cards with **magnetic strips**, such as credit cards and gift cards. The magnets can erase the information that is coded on the strip.

Magnetic Attraction

Steps to follow

1 Test the items you collected to see if they are attracted to your magnet. Divide your objects into three piles:
 a) Things that are attracted strongly to the magnet;
 b) Things that are attracted weakly to the magnet;
 c) Things that are not attracted to the magnet.

What does a magnet attract?

For this activity you will need:
* A magnet
* An assortment of metal objects such as coins, clips, eating utensils, nails, jewelry, and aluminum foil.

Something more

Go on a magnet hunt! Take your magnet into different rooms in your home. Which things are attracted to the magnet? Try metal handles and knobs, bed frames, chairs, and metal furniture. If you have a strong magnet, you might be able to find places on the wall that are attracted to your magnet. This is because there are studs, or nails, in the frame of your home. Remember not to try anything that is electrical. You could get hurt, and the magnet could damage the electrical device.

Minerals and magnets

Some kinds of minerals are also attracted to magnets. Two of these include hematite, which is a shiny black or reddish color stone that is sometimes used in jewelry, and magnetite, which is a mineral that contains iron. **Lodestone** is a type of magnetite. These minerals are attracted to magnets because they contain iron. If you have access to a rock collection, you may want to test the rocks with your magnet.

Black sand is often attracted to magnets.

Magnets at the beach

Some kinds of sand are attracted to magnets. The next time you go to the beach or playground, take a magnet and a plastic bag along. Put the magnet in the bag to keep sand from getting onto your magnet. Dip your bag-covered magnet into the sand. Does any of it stick? You can save your magnetic sand by gently shaking the magnet to get the non-magnetic sand off. Then, hold the bag over a container and gently remove the magnet. The sand should fall into your container. You can use magnetic sand for some of the experiments in this book!

Steps to follow

For this activity you will need:
* A small metal paper clip
* Thread
* Scissors
* Tape
* A strong magnet
* Table.

1 Cut a piece of thread about 12 in (30 cm) long. Tie one end to a paper clip. Tape the other end to the top of a table or desk, about 6 in (15 cm) away from a wall.

2 Tape the magnet on the wall so that when you bring the paper clip toward it, the paper clip almost touches it. You should be able to feel the paper clip being attracted to the magnet. The thread will be tight and slanted toward the wall. Tape the magnet to the wall at that spot.

3 Bring the paper clip close to the magnet again. When you let the paper clip go, it should float just below the magnet!

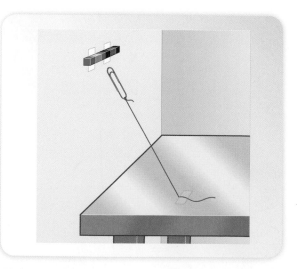

Warning: Ask an adult before sticking a magnet to the wall.

8

What is happening?

The magnet is attracting the paper clip, but the paper clip cannot stick to the magnet because the thread holds it back. The magnetic force is stronger than **gravity**, so the paper clip floats just below the magnet. What do you think would happen if you cut the thread? Would the paper clip fall down to the table or stick to the magnet? Try it!

You can fool your friends by setting up the same experiment. This time put the magnet behind a poster or a picture you have drawn. Your friends will not know why the paper clip is floating! Magnetic forces can travel through paper, plastic, and even water!

Magnets can hold things to a refrigerator because magnetic forces go through paper.

Magnetic boats

Tape a paper clip to a Styrofoam packing peanut. Float the peanut in a plastic bowl of water. Use a magnet under the bowl to move your boat. Try using two boats. What if you make the water deeper—will the magnet still work? What happens if you use a metal bowl?

Why are only some metals attracted to magnets?

The metals that are attracted to magnets are iron, cobalt, and nickel. Steel and other **alloys** made with these metals may also be attracted to magnets. An alloy is a metal that is made up of either two or more metals or a metal and another material. Steel is an alloy of iron and carbon.

Like all **matter**, metal is made from **atoms**. Atoms contain many **electrons**, which circle (orbit) around a **nucleus**. Each electron consists of a small electronic charge (force). In most substances the electrons are paired. The paired electrons move in opposite directions, so they cancel each other out and do not make a charge.

In **magnetic materials** there are a lot of unpaired electrons. The charges of these unpaired electrons cause some of the atoms to line themselves up with nearby atoms. This means that the atoms move until they all face the same direction. When all of the atoms in a section are aligned, they create a magnetic area called a **magnetic domain**.

There are many magnetic domains in a single piece of metal. Even though the atoms within the magnetic domains are facing one direction, the domains themselves are not lined up with each other. They face in random directions.

Magnetic material contains magnetic domains. In a magnet, all the magnetic domains face the same way.

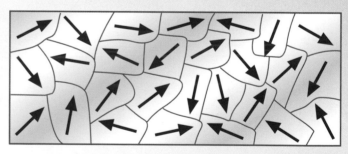

iron

Magnetic cars

A car probably has over 20 magnets—everything from the ignition system to the windshield wipers needs a magnet!

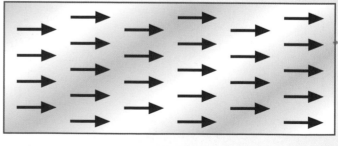

magnet

How do magnets work?

In a magnet all the atoms in the metal are aligned, making one large magnetic domain. The charges from all those lined up atoms create a magnetic force. The more electrons that are lined up, the stronger the magnet is.

Magnetic cows

Farmers sometimes have cows swallow magnets! The magnet is heavy, so it stays at the bottom of the cow's stomach. It is also strong enough to attract any metal that the cow might ingest, such as old cans or wire. The magnet keeps the metal from damaging the cow's insides.

Magnetic Fields

Steps to follow

Seeing magnetic fields

For this activity you will need:
* A clear bottle of baby oil
* Iron filings, magnetic sand, or fibers from fine steel wool
* A variety of magnets.

1 Take the label off the bottle of baby oil. You may need to soak it in hot water.

2 Add about a tablespoon of **iron filings** or magnetic sand to the bottle of oil. If you are using steel wool, tear it over a container to get small fibers to come out. You will have to tear it quite a bit to get enough fibers. Put the cap back on the bottle. Make sure to screw it on tightly!

3 Shake the bottle to distribute the filings through the oil. Press a magnet to the side of the bottle. Watch as the filings are drawn to the magnet. Shake the bottle again to redistribute the filings and try different magnets. Try moving the magnets along the side of the bottle. What happens if you try two magnets?

Something more

Take a small bar magnet and wrap it tightly in plastic wrap. Tie it to the end of a piece of string and carefully dip it into the bottle. You may need to pour a small amount of baby oil out first to keep the bottle from overflowing when you put the magnet in. The filings will cling to the magnet, and you will be able to see the whole **magnetic field**!

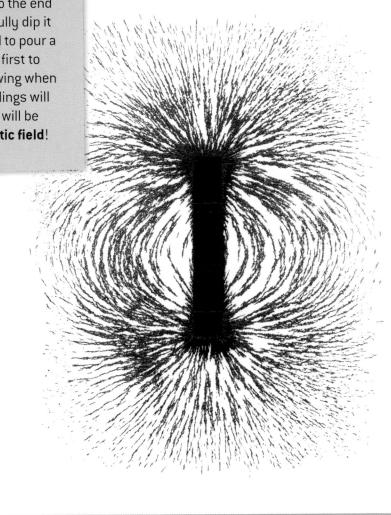

These iron filings show the lines in the magnet's magnetic field.

Magnetic art

You can save a picture of a magnetic field! Place a bar magnet under a piece of white paper. Gently sprinkle iron filings, magnetic sand, or steel wool fibers over the paper. Spread white glue on another piece of paper. It should be thick, but not dripping. Gently press the paper, glue side down, onto the filings. When you pick the paper back up again, some of the filings should be stuck to it in the pattern of the magnetic field!

Magnetic patterns

A magnetic field is the region around the magnet that attracts **magnetic material**. Magnetic fields are invisible, but you can see how they are formed when you use iron filings. You probably noticed that more filings were attracted to the **poles**. That is because the magnetic field is strongest at the poles. The lines of the magnetic field are always curved. If you look carefully, you will see that each line forms a complete loop, and these loops never cross each other.

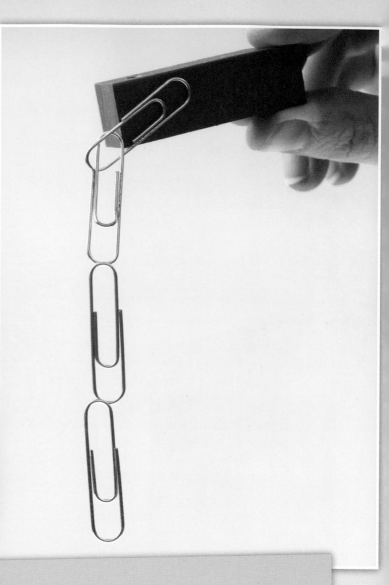

These paper clips have become temporary magnets.

Powerful magnetic fields

As you saw with the iron filings experiment, magnetic fields extend beyond the magnet. Stronger magnets have magnetic fields that extend farther. When iron or steel comes into contact with a magnetic field, it is not only attracted to the magnet but also becomes a **temporary magnet** itself.

You can prove this by dipping a magnet into a container of paper clips. Many of the paper clips will stick to the magnet, but some of the paper clips will stick to other paper clips without touching the magnet themselves. The paper clips are attracting other paper clips because they have become temporary magnets as a result of being in the magnetic field. See how far your magnet's magnetic field extends by trying to make a chain of paper clips. Can you see how the field gets weaker as you get farther from the magnet?

Make a magnetic sculpture

You can make a sculpture using the power of a magnetic field! Tape a strong magnet under a small paper plate. Put a handful of small steel objects such as ball bearings, washers, or nuts on top of the plate. Make the objects into a sculpture. Your sculpture is being held together by a magnetic field! What will happen to your sculpture if you hold another magnet near it? What if you remove the magnet from underneath the plate?

This sculpture is being held together by magnetic forces.

Hunting for magnetic fields

Magnets are in all kinds of things, from CD players to refrigerators. This means that magnetic fields are common in our environment. Because they are very weak, we cannot feel them. See if you can find some magnetic fields by taking a walk with a **compass**. Watch the needle of the compass carefully. Normally, the needle of a compass points north, but when it comes in contact with a magnetic field, it will point toward the field. You can test this by putting your compass near a magnet. What happens when you put your compass near an electronic device? If the needle points toward the device, it probably contains a magnet!

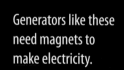

Generators like these need magnets to make electricity.

Magnetic fields in power plants

Did you know that you could not turn on an electric light if there were no magnets? Magnets are used in **generators** to make electricity. Inside a generator there are strong magnets. These magnets create a powerful magnetic field. Inside the magnetic field are coils of copper wire. When the magnet or the copper wires move, the magnetic field produces an electric **current** in the copper wire. This current is electricity!

Generators can be very small. Some handheld generators produce just enough electricity to power a flashlight or radio. Large generators in power plants produce enough electricity to power thousands of houses!

Horseshoe magnets are stronger than bar magnets because the poles are close together.

Increasing the magnetic field

A magnetic field can be increased if the poles of the magnet are close together. If you have been experimenting with a horseshoe magnet, you have probably discovered that the poles are on the ends, not on the curve. That is because a horseshoe magnet is really just a bar magnet that has been bent into a "U" shape. A bar magnet can be made stronger by bending it into a horseshoe shape because when the poles are close together, the strength of the magnetic field around them increases.

Earth's Magnetic Field

Steps to follow

Make a compass

For this activity you will need:

* A Styrofoam cup
* Scissors
* A steel sewing needle
* A bar magnet
* Glue or tape
* A small bowl of water (not metal)
* A pen.

1 Rub the needle 50 times in one direction with the magnet. This will make the needle into a magnet.

2 Cut the bottom out of the cup so that you have a circle. Glue or tape the needle to the Styrofoam circle.

3 Put the Styrofoam circle in the bowl of water. The foam circle should turn until one end of the needle points north and the other points south. You may need to use a real **compass** to figure out which end of the needle is pointing north. Once you know which end of the needle is pointing north, you can use a pen to mark the Styrofoam near that end with an "N." Put an "S" at the other end of the needle for "south." Can you figure out where on the Styrofoam circle you should mark west and east?

How does it work?

When you rubbed the needle with the magnet, it caused the **magnetic domains** inside the needle to line up, and it became a magnet, too. The magnetized needle naturally aligned itself with Earth's **magnetic field** to point north. Just putting the needle on the table would not have worked because the magnetic force is not strong enough to move the needle when there is so much **friction**. But the needle could move more easily in water because there is less friction.

The needle of a compass always points to magnetic north.

If you want to use your compass outside, put the Styrofoam circle into a small container, like a jar lid filled with water, and cover it with plastic wrap to keep the water in. A **petri dish** will also work well. Watch as the needle readjusts to point north every time you move the compass.

Magnetic Earth

The biggest magnet in the world actually is Earth! Earth itself is a magnet. This is because the outer **core** of Earth is made of liquid iron and nickel. Scientists believe the rotation of Earth interacts with the liquid iron and nickel in the core of the planet to create a magnetic field. One way to imagine this is to picture Earth with a giant bar magnet running through the center. Just like any other magnetic field, Earth's magnetic field is strongest at the **poles**. This is why the ends of your needle were drawn to Earth's magnetic poles.

Spinning needle

If you try to use a compass at the magnetic north pole, the needle will spin freely. The same thing will happen if you use a compass at the magnetic south pole. This is because at the poles, the needle is pulled downward. Since it cannot actually point down, it ends up spinning—unless you tilt the compass.

Geographic north and magnetic north are not located in the same place.

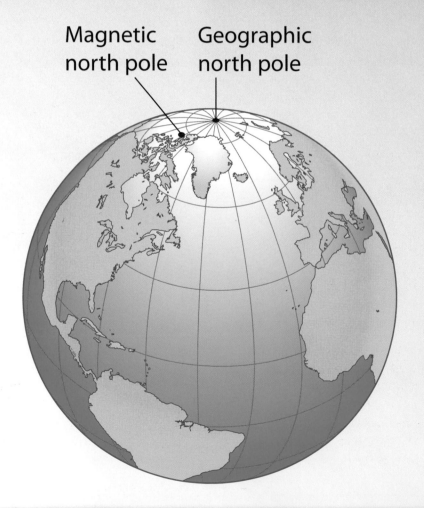

Magnetic north pole   Geographic north pole

Magnetic sense in animals

Scientists believe that some animals, including migrating birds and sea turtles, can sense Earth's magnetic field and use it for **navigation**. Scientists believe that this is possible because these animals have small amounts of the mineral magnetite in their bodies.

Magnetic north

Your compass does not actually point to the North Pole. It points to **magnetic north**. Magnetic north is currently located in northern Canada, about 1,000 miles (1,600 km) away from the real North Pole. Because the liquid core at the center of Earth is always moving, magnetic north also moves. It is currently moving about 6 miles (10 km) every year toward Siberia, but that could change. The movement of the magnetic poles is unpredictable. Some scientists even believe that the poles of Earth have switched—maybe even many times.

Steps to follow

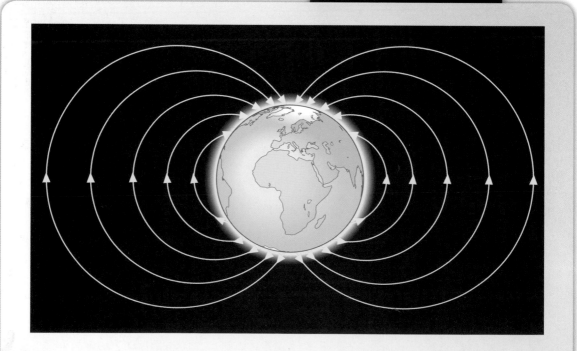

1 You can use Earth's magnetic field to tell which end of a magnet is the north pole and which end is the south pole. Tie a string around the center of a magnet and hang it so that the poles are balanced.

2 Tape the other end of the string to the edge of a table so the magnet hangs in the air. Just like your compass needle, the magnet will turn until the north end is facing magnetic north.

Finding the poles

For this activity you will need:

* A magnet
* String
* Tape
* A marker
* A table.

3 Once you know which end of the magnet is the north pole, you can write on it with a marker.

The Earth's magnetic field extends far into space.

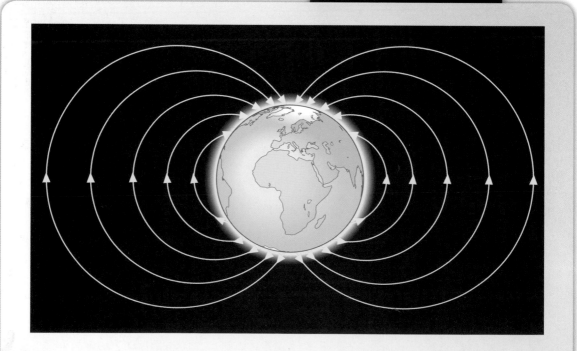

What is happening?

You know that magnetic poles are attracted to their opposites. You may be wondering why the north pole of a magnet is attracted to the magnetic north pole rather than to the magnetic south pole. The magnetic poles of a magnet are called "north seeking" and "south seeking." This means that the north pole end of a magnet "seeks" the magnetic north pole of Earth.

Lodestone compass

Before compasses were invented, people hung **lodestones** from string to find north. Because lodestone is magnetized, it also points north.

The northern lights are caused by particles that are drawn to the Earth by its magnetic field.

Magnetic fields in space

Earth's magnetic field extends about 36,000 miles (57,900 km) into space. It protects our planet from dangerous **solar winds**. Solar winds are streams of fast-moving charged **particles** that come from the Sun. Although Earth's magnetic field deflects most of the solar wind, some particles do get through. These particles are drawn toward the poles by Earth's magnetic field. When they hit Earth's atmosphere, they create the beautiful display of lights called the **northern lights**, or **aurora borealis**, that can often be seen in Alaska and other northern regions. Occasionally, they can even be seen in southern Canada and in the northern United States.

Attracting and Repelling

Steps to follow

1 Tie a piece of string to the center of one of the bar magnets. Make sure the magnet is balanced and that one pole is not slanting toward the floor.

2 Tape the other end of the string to a table so that the magnet can swing freely.

3 Take the other magnet in your hand. Slowly, bring the north pole of this magnet close to the south pole of the hanging magnet. What happened?

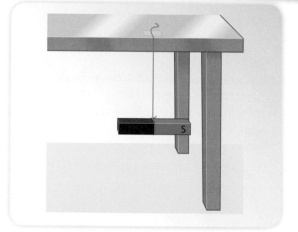

4 Now try to touch the north pole of the hanging magnet with the north pole of the magnet in your hand. Could you do it? What happened? Can you make the hanging magnet spin without touching it?

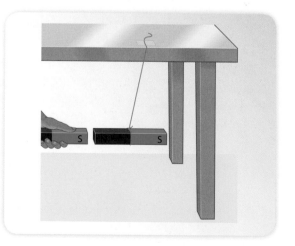

Opposites attract

The north and south poles of your magnets were attracted to each other. That is why the hanging magnet seemed to jump to the magnet in your hand. But when you tried to touch like poles together, they **repelled** each other. That is why you could not touch the like poles together.

Try tying a second bar magnet on a string and hang it near the first one. How do the two magnets interact? What if you add a third magnet?

Opposite poles on a pair of magnets are attracted to each other.

Feel the force

Hold two round or doughnut-shaped magnets close together with their opposite poles facing, but do not let them touch. Can you feel the attracting force? Now turn one of the magnets around and try to put the two magnets together. Can you feel the repelling force?

Now put one of the magnets on the table and hold the other magnet above it. Can you make the magnet on the table jump to the one in your hand? Can you use the one in your hand to move the magnet on the table without touching it?

Crazy magnet

For this activity you will need:

* A ruler or other stick
* Clear tape
* A doughnut-shaped magnet
* Four round or doughnut-shaped magnets
* Thread or string
* A table.

1 Tape the four round magnets on the floor in a square about 6 in (15 cm) from the edge of a table. The magnets should be spaced about 2 in (5 cm) away from each other.

2 Tape the ruler onto the table so that it extends over the four magnets.

3 Tie the doughnut-shaped magnet to a piece of thread. Tie the other end of the thread to the ruler. Make the thread long enough so that the hanging magnet interacts with the **magnetic fields** of the magnets on the floor. Swing the hanging magnet gently over the taped magnets and see what happens.

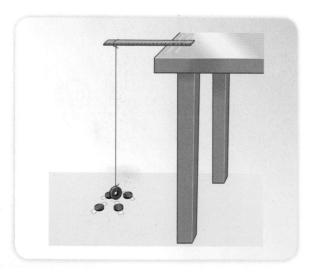

What is happening?

The magnetic fields of both the hanging magnet and the ones that are taped to the floor are interacting to make the hanging magnet move in strange and unpredictable ways. One second the hanging magnet is being repelled, and the next it is being attracted. The attracting and repelling forces keep the magnet swinging.

Try changing the design of the magnets on the floor. Does it matter if the poles that face up are all the same? Try adding more magnets. What if you use different shapes of magnets?

Magnet pieces

If you cut a magnet in half, both pieces will have a north and a south pole. Even if you cut a very small piece off the magnet, it will still have both poles.

Repelling forces keep these magnets floating.

Floating magnets

Put doughnut magnets on a pencil with opposite poles facing each other. The repelling forces will make the magnets float and bounce. Try pressing all of the magnets down and then letting go. Can you use the repelling forces to pop the top magnet off the pencil?

Maglev trains

Magnetic levitation trains, called **maglev** trains for short, use the power of repelling magnets. Maglev trains have magnets on their underside as well as on the track. The magnets repel each other to keep the train floating about 6 in (15 cm) above the track. The repelling forces also move the train forward. Because there is very little **friction**, these trains can move very fast—over 300 mph (480 kmh). This is as fast as a jet airplane!

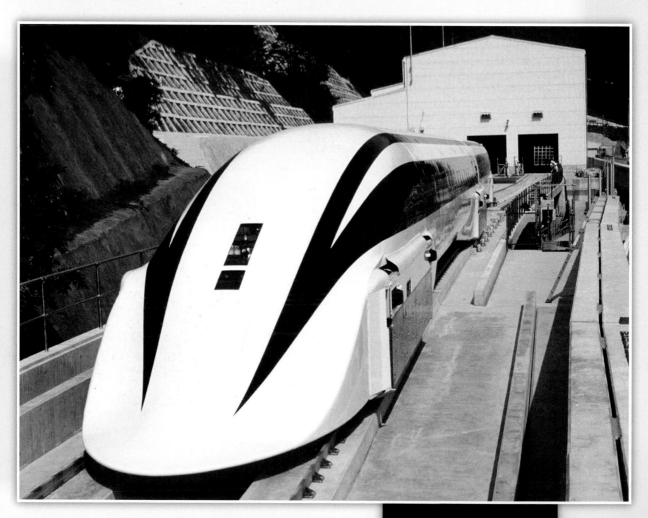

Maglev trains are an exciting technology, but they are expensive to build and difficult to maintain. Currently, there are maglev trains in Germany and Japan. Maglev train lines may soon be built in other countries, including the United States.

This maglev train can reach speeds of over 300 mph (480 kmh).

Roller coasters

Did you know that magnets are used in some roller coasters? Many roller coasters now use magnets to slow down and stop. Magnets are placed on both the coaster and the track. As the coaster moves over the magnets, the attracting forces slow it to a gentle stop.

Many roller coasters use magnets to help stop the coaster.

Some newer roller coasters begin the ride with a rapid **acceleration**, rather than with a gradual climb up a hill. Many of these roller coasters are using the power of repelling magnets to get this speedy start. The California Screamin' roller coaster at Disney's California Adventure theme park begins with a heart-stopping race to the top of the first hill that reaches a speed of 55 mph (89 kmh) in just 4 seconds! Another ride that uses magnet technology for acceleration is the Wicked Twister at the Cedar Point theme park in Sandusky, Ohio. This attraction uses magnets to launch riders up to the top of a twisted U-shaped track at speeds of up to 72 mph (116 kmh). **Gravity** brings them down again, but as soon as they reach the bottom, they are launched upward again to the other side of the U!

Making Magnets

Steps to follow

Magnetizing metal

For this activity you will need:

* A magnet
* A steel knitting needle
* Paper clips.

1 Try to use the knitting needle as a magnet. Can you use it to pick up any paper clips?

2 Rub the magnet along the knitting needle at least 50 times. Use just one pole of the magnet to rub the needle. Rub in only one direction, not back and forth.

3 Try using the knitting needle as a magnet again. Can you pick up any paper clips now?

What happened?

Remember that **magnetic materials** such as steel contain **magnetic domains** in which all the **atoms** are aligned to face one direction. When you rubbed the steel needle with the magnet, the magnetic domains were attracted to the magnet and were pulled in the direction of the stroke. When enough domains face in one direction, the metal becomes a magnet.

You can make your magnet stronger by rubbing it more times. Try magnetizing an iron nail. Which magnet works the best?

Three kinds of magnets

Magnets can be classified into three categories. **Permanent magnets** are like the ones on your refrigerator. They remain magnets. They do not lose their magnetism unless they are damaged.

Temporary magnets cannot keep their magnetic power. The magnet you just made is a temporary magnet—it will eventually lose its magnetism. A metal object such as a paper clip that is in a **magnetic field** is also a temporary magnet. It will lose its magnetic ability as soon as the magnetic field is taken away.

Rubbing a nail against the pole of a magnet will make the nail into a temporary magnet. The nail will then pick up other magnetic materials.

Mixing up the domains

You can make your temporary magnet weaker by jiggling it. The motion jiggles the domains out of alignment, so the magnet loses strength.

Electromagnets use electricity to make a magnet. Electrical **current** is used to align the magnetic domains. Unlike other magnets, electromagnets can be turned on and off.

Steps to follow

Make an electromagnet

For this activity you will need:

* A large iron nail
* A fresh D-size battery
* 3 feet (90 cm) of thin insulated wire
* Wire strippers
* Tape
* Paper clips.

1 Ask an adult to strip about 1 in (2.5 cm) of the plastic coating off the ends of the wire.

2 Wrap the wire around the nail as many times as you can. Leave about 1 in (2.5 cm) at the end of the nail without wire. Also, leave about 8 in (20 cm) of wire on each end of the coil. You might have to cut the wire to get the right length. If you do, be sure to ask an adult to strip plastic coating off the new end of the wire.

3 Tape the ends of the wires to the ends of the battery.

4 See if you can pick up some paper clips with the end of the nail. Be careful—the nail and the exposed wires may get hot!

Warning: Adult help may be needed for this experiment.

How it works

The electric current from the battery creates a magnetic field in the wire coils. This electric current magnetizes the nail. The wire does not have to be made from magnetic material, but it does need to be able to **conduct** electricity. You can turn your electromagnet off by disconnecting one of the wires from the battery.

This electromagnet is being used to move scrap metal at a recycling center.

More with your electromagnet

How can you make your electromagnet stronger? Try adding another battery. Try wrapping the coil more times around the nail. What if you use something other than a nail for the core? Try a screwdriver, a knitting needle, or a chopstick. Can you think of a way to make a switch to turn your electromagnet on and off?

Just like in earlier experiments, you can use **iron filings**, magnetic sand, or steel wool fibers to show the magnetic field that your electromagnet creates. Just put your electromagnet under a piece of paper and sprinkle the filings on top.

Using electromagnets

Electromagnets have many uses. This is because the electricity can make them more powerful than ordinary magnets, and also because they can be turned on and off. Electromagnets are used in many household appliances and electronics. One common use of electromagnets is in speakers. Inside a speaker a permanent magnet and an electromagnet form a magnetic field. Electricity is used to constantly reverse the **poles** on the electromagnet. When the poles switch, it causes a disruption in the magnetic field, which makes vibrations. These vibrations can be made into sound.

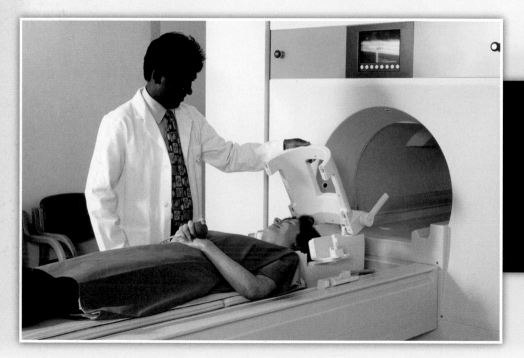

MRI machines use powerful electromagnets to help diagnose illnesses and injuries.

Medical uses for electromagnets

Many medical devices use magnets. Some of the most well known are large scanners that perform **magnetic resonance imaging (MRI)**. MRI devices use powerful doughnut-shaped electromagnets to create a magnetic field around a patient's body. The charges in the atoms in the patient's body respond to the magnetic field. Computers measure the reactions and make them into pictures. These pictures can be used by doctors to diagnose illness and injuries. MRIs can be used to diagnose diseases such as cancer or a heart condition. They can also help a doctor determine if a person is bleeding internally or if the patient's organs are damaged. Many lives have been saved because of MRI technology.

Magnets are used in particle accelerators like this one so that physicists can study atoms.

Electromagnets in research

Scientists use electromagnets to study atoms. Electromagnetic fields can be used to make atoms move at high speeds in giant circular tubes called **particle accelerators**. These tubes can be many miles long. The atoms race through the tube until they are going extremely fast. **Physicists** then smash the atoms together and study what they do. A great deal has been learned about atoms from performing these experiments.

The world's largest particle accelerator is located in both France and Switzerland. It is over 16 miles (27 km) long. This giant particle accelerator uses thousands of magnets to push atoms to nearly the speed of light, which is nearly 200 million miles (320 million km) per second!

Motor Power

Steps to follow

1 Use the rubber band to secure the safety pins to the ends of the battery. The ends of the safety pins with the loops should be facing straight up and the fasteners should be touching the negative and positive terminals of the battery.

2 Put the magnet on the battery between the two safety pins. The battery case is made from steel, so the magnet will stick.

3 Wrap the wire around the permanent marker five to seven times. You should have at least 6 in (15 cm) of extra wire on each end. Carefully take the wire coil off the marker. Wrap the extra wire around the coil one or two times in order to secure it. The extra wire should extend about 2 in (5 cm) out from each side. The wires must be directly across from each other. If the coil were the face of a clock, the wires would stick out at 3 o'clock and 9 o'clock.

Make a simple electric motor

For this activity you will need:
* A fresh D-size battery
* A small magnet
* Two large metal safety pins
* A rubber band
* A permanent black marker
* About 2 feet (90 cm) of thin enamel insulated copper wire, sometimes called magnetic wire. (You can use insulated wire if you don't have magnetic wire.)
* Fine sandpaper.

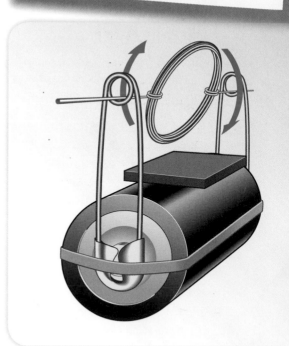

Warning: Adult help may be needed for this experiment.

4 Use the sandpaper to scrape off all the enamel on the ends of the wires. If you are using insulated wire, strip the ends of the wires.

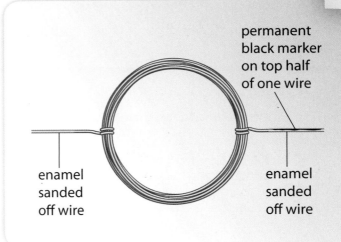

permanent black marker on top half of one wire

enamel sanded off wire

enamel sanded off wire

5 Use the black permanent marker to color the top half of one of the wires. Be sure that you do not color all the way around the wire (see page 40 to find out why).

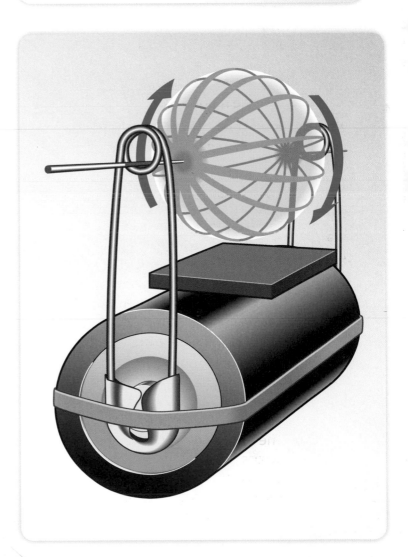

6 Put the ends of the wires through the loops in the safety pins so that the wire coil is suspended over the magnet. Give the circle a little push to start it off. It should spin quickly on its own after that!

Getting your motor to work

If your coil does not spin, try some of these suggestions:

- Make sure all your connections are tight. Be especially sure that the safety pins are touching the negative and positive ends of the battery.

- Make sure the coil is balanced. Try adjusting the wires that come out from the coil so that they are directly across from each other.

- Make sure the wire coil is directly over the **permanent magnet**. The wire coil must also be close enough to the permanent magnet so that their **magnetic fields** interact. You may need to adjust the safety pins to get the coil closer to the permanent magnet.

- Make sure that you have not colored both the top and the bottom of the wire with black ink. If you think you have too much black ink on the wire, sand it all off and color the top of the wire again.

Motors make things such as this fan spin.

The first motor

Physicist Michael Faraday invented the first motor in 1821. Faraday's motor made a magnet move to demonstrate how electricity could be transformed into a different form of energy—energy that moves!

This propeller is being powered by a powerful motor.

More with your motor

Can you improve your **motor**? Try using a different permanent magnet. What if you make a wire circle with more coils or make the coils bigger?

Try to make your motor into a small fan. Make a propeller from a piece of paper or other very light material like balsa wood. Attach the propeller to the ends of one of the wires that sticks out from the loop in the safety pin. When the coil spins, the propeller will also spin!

You can use your motor to lift a very light object. Tie a piece of thread to the coil. Put a piece of O-shaped cereal or another light object on the other end of the thread. As the motor turns, it will wind the thread up and move the cereal toward the motor!

How your electric motor works

A motor turns electrical energy into mechanical energy (motion). The electrical energy comes from the battery. When the coil of copper wire is connected to the battery with the safety pins, it becomes an **electromagnet**. One face of the coil becomes the south **pole** and the other becomes the north pole. The permanent magnet that you put on the battery attracts its opposite pole and **repels** its like pole, causing the coil to spin.

These large motors are inside a big ship.

You may be wondering why you had to color the top half of one of the wires with black marker. As the coil turns, the black ink acts as an insulator and stops the flow of electricity for half of every turn. If the electricity did not stop, the wire coil would get stuck when the opposite sides of the magnets were facing each other. For example, if the north pole of the permanent magnet were facing up, then when the south pole of the coil faced it, the coil would stop moving. It would be held in place by the magnetic attraction. But since there is no power for half of each spin, this does not happen. **Momentum** keeps the coil turning until the **current** flows again.

Millions of motors

Motors are all around us. There are small motors in household appliances such as blenders and computers. Larger motors are found in vehicles. There are motors as large as cars that are used to power large machinery. The biggest motors power large cargo ships. These motors can weigh as much as 2,300 tons (2087 tonnes) and use over 1,600 gallons (6057 litres) of oil each hour!

Nanomotors

The smallest motors are 250 times smaller than a human hair. These tiny motors, called nanomotors, may be used in the future for communication and medical technologies.

This nanomotor is 250 times smaller than a human hair.

Magnificent Magnets

Magnets are used billions of times every day. Our lives would be very different without them. Not only would we not be able to stick artwork to our refrigerators easily, but we would also have trouble keeping the refrigerator door closed. A **magnetic strip** around the door keeps it sealed! We also could not generate electricity. There would be no cars or airplanes, because **motors** would be impossible without magnets. Anything with a speaker, such as a telephone or amplifier, would not work. Finding north would be more challenging as well. In addition, there would be no way to use a bank's automatic teller machine (ATM), because there would be no magnetic strip on the cash card for the machine to read.

Magnets have helped us learn about ourselves and our world. Powerful **electromagnets** are essential in the study of **atoms**. Magnets also help us to learn more about our bodies. Magnets are used in **MRI** devices to diagnose illnesses and injuries. MRI technology continues to improve doctors' ability to save more and more lives. Many technologies that we depend on every day use magnets!

This speaker uses magnets to amplify the sound from the guitar.

The body's magnetic field

The cells in the human body generate electromagnetic **currents**, giving the body a weak magnetic field.

Here magnets are being used to treat this person for rheumatism.

Magnets in action

People continue to find new and clever ways to use magnets. The attracting forces of magnets can be used to hold giant pieces of steel in a factory so that clamps are not needed. They can also be used to take microscopic pieces of **mineral** out of drinking water. Factories that package food use magnets to make sure that tiny pieces of metal do not get in the food. **Repelling** magnetic forces can be used to levitate (raise up) dangerous materials in labs so that scientists can observe and manipulate them without touching them. Magnets are even being used to study how some liquids behave in space. New technologies are sure to bring exciting new uses for magnets in the future.

Glossary

acceleration change in the speed or direction of an object. Magnets can be used to start a roller coaster with rapid acceleration.

alloy substance that is made of two or more metals. Alloys are made by mixing the metals when they are still in a liquid form.

atom extremely tiny particle. Atoms make up all things.

aurora borealis see "northern lights"

compass navigational tool that uses a magnetic needle to point north. It is a good idea to carry a compass and a map with you when you are out hiking.

conduct allow electricity, sound, or heat to pass. Wires are made from metal because metal conducts electricity.

core center of Earth made of very hot iron. Part of it is liquid and part is solid.

current flow of electricity

electromagnet magnet that is created when electricity flows through a coil of wire wrapped around a metal core. An electromagnet can be made much stronger than an ordinary magnet.

electron tiny charged particle

friction the rubbing of two objects against each other. A maglev train can move very fast because there is no friction from the tracks.

generator machine that converts motion into electrical energy. Generators use magnets to create an electrical current.

gravity force that keeps everything on Earth

iron filing very small piece of iron

lodestone naturally magnetic rock. A lodestone contains iron.

maglev magnetic levitation; a technology that uses the repelling forces of magnets to suspend an object

magnetic domain small area on a piece of magnetic material on which all the atoms are facing in one direction. There are many magnetic domains in even a small piece of iron.

magnetic field area around a magnet in which a magnetic force acts

magnetic material substance, such as steel, that is attracted to magnets

magnetic north direction that a compass will point as the needle lines up with the Earth's magnetic field

magnetic resonance imaging (MRI) technology for producing images of organs by measuring how the body responds to a strong magnetic field. The magnets in a magnetic resonance imaging device are so strong that they must be shielded so they do not attract magnetic material around them.

magnetic strip strip of magnetic material on the back of credit, ATM, and gift cards on which information can be stored. You should keep magnets away from the magnetic strip on a credit card.

matter anything that has weight and takes up space. Everything you see, including yourself, is made from matter.

mineral substance that occurs naturally in rocks. Some minerals, such as magnetite, are magnetic.

momentum how an object in motion tends to keep moving. Momentum keeps your bike moving forward, even if you stop pedaling.

motor device that turns electrical energy into motion. You can use a small motor to make a model car.

navigation plotting a course from one place to another. The invention of the compass made navigation much easier on long voyages.

northern lights (aurora borealis) colored display of lights that is caused by particles from the Sun that get caught in Earth's magnetic field. The northern lights can also sometimes be seen in northern parts of the United States.

nucleus center of an atom

particles tiny piece of something

particle accelerator machine that uses powerful electromagnets to move atoms at high speeds so that they can be smashed and studied

permanent magnet magnet that does not lose its magnetic ability unless it is damaged. You can weaken a permanent magnet by striking it with a hammer.

petri dish shallow, circular clear dish with a flat lid

physicist scientist who studies force, motion, matter, and energy

poles places on a magnet where the magnetic force is the strongest

repel force that pushes objects away from each other. You can move a magnet without touching it by making one magnet repel another magnet.

solar wind fast-moving stream of particles that comes from the Sun. Earth's magnetic field protects us from dangerous solar winds.

temporary magnet magnet that will lose its magnetic ability over time. You can make a stainless steel spoon into a temporary magnet by rubbing it with a permanent magnet.

Find Out More

Books

Gardner, Robert. *Energizing Science Projects with Electricity and Magnetism*. Berkeley Heights, N.J.: Enslow Elementary, 2006.

This book gives instructions and suggestions for science fair projects.

Lauw, Darlene. *Magnets (Science Alive!)*. New York: Crabtree, 2002.

This book offers experiments, background information, and fun facts and quizzes.

Rohrig, Brian. *39 Amazing Experiments with the Mega-Magnet*. Plain City, Ohio: FizzBang Science, 2003.

This book comes with a mega-magnet, one of the most powerful magnets on the planet, and contains dozens of illustrated experiments.

Whyman, Kathryn. *Electricity and Magnetism (Science World)*. Mankato, Minn.: Stargazer, 2005.

This book includes experiments and background information on electricity and magnetism.

Websites

Exploratorium: Science Snacks About Magnetism

www.exploratorium.edu/snacks/iconmagnetism.html

A collection of experiments from San Francisco's Exploratorium science museum. Includes step-by-step instructions, pictures, and plenty of background information.

How Magnets Work

www.howmagnetswork.com

This website has a wealth of information about magnets, including history, uses, and types.

Organizations

The American Association for the Advancement of Science (AAAS)
1200 New York Avenue NW
Washington, D.C. 20005
(202) 326-6400
www.aaas.org/

An international nonprofit organization dedicated to advancing science around the world.

The Vega Science Trust
Sussex Innovation Centre
Science Park Square
Brighton, BN1 9SB
United Kingdom
+44 -1273 678726
www.vega.org.uk/

A nonprofit trust that broadcasts science programs for free over the Internet.

Places to visit

The Bakken
3537 Zenith Avenue South
Minneapolis, Minn. 55416
(612) 926-3878
www.thebakken.org
This hands-on museum focuses exclusively on electricity and magnetism.

Fermilab
P.O. Box 500
Batavia, Ill. 60510-5011
(630) 840-3000
www.fnal.gov

Visit Fermilab and see and learn about a real particle accelerator! You can also visit the Lederman Science Center, where you can learn more about atoms and how they relate to magnets.

Index